BEN SHAHN: THE PASSION OF SACCO AND VANZETTI

First Edition

BEN SHAHN: THE PASSION OF SACCO AND VANZETTI

By

MARTIN H BUSH

With An Essay And Commentary By

BEN SHAHN

SYRACUSE UNIVERSITY | 1968

Dedicated to the memory of

RICHARD EVANS III

October 20, 1941 | July 16, 1965

CONTENTS

DIMENSIONS ARE GIVEN IN INCHES, HEIGHT PRECEDING WIDTH, UNLESS OTHERWISE INDICATED.

ACKNOWLEDGEMENTS

My obligations in this undertaking are manifold. I wish to express my sincere gratitude to Mr. and Mrs. Jacob Schulman and Mr. and Mrs. Richard Evans II who made the Sacco-Vanzetti Mural possible through their generous and unfailing support; to Ben Shahn, not only for his mural and his essay, but also for the unselfish help and cooperation he has given me during the past three years; and to Martin Fass and Richard Wilson for their thoughtful suggestions.

Most of all I am grateful to Vice-President Frank P. Piskor of Syracuse University, who, by example and deed, has always been an inspiration to me in my work.

I would also like to thank those who through correspondence, conversation, advice, or material support, have sustained and encouraged me, and for these kindnesses I owe particular debts of gratitude to the following: Chancellor William Pearson Tolley, Dean James R. Manwaring, and Dean Lawrence Schmeckebier of Syracuse University, Edward S. Amazeen, Moses Asch, Gerald L. Barsha, Harry Bosch, Mr. and Mrs. George Brewster, Bernarda Bryson, J. Lionberger Davis, Virginia Denton, Leon Despres, Candace DeSilvey, Frank Dudziak, Donald P. Ely, Martha Holt, Horace M. Kallen, Robert Kearns, Elaine Kenyon, Lincoln Kirstein, Gladys Leiter, Goddard Lieberson, Mr. and Mrs. Gabriel Loire, Loire Imports, Inc., John M. Nolan, Austin G. Paulnack, James Thrall Soby, Katherine Stadler, Peter Tarolli, Edward M. M. Warburg and F. Palmer Weber.

Illustrations for this book were supplied by: Robert T. Elson, Time-Life Books, Inc.; Edith Gregor Halpert, The Downtown Gallery; Patricia M. Healy, Frances Follin Jones, Princeton University; Mr. and Mrs. Samuel Porter, Ben Shahn, Richard Tooke, Museum of Modern Art; United Press International, Philip Wittenberg and Rudolf G. Wunderlich, Kennedy Galleries.

Responsibility for this book is borne by me. Syracuse University is not to be held accountable for any errors or opinions in the text.

Martin H. Bush
May, 1968

8   On August 23, 1927, two convicted murderers, Nicola Sacco and Bartolomeo Vanzetti, died for a crime many people believed they did not commit. Forty years later, almost to the day, artist Ben Shahn once again focused attention on their controversial trial with a magnificent mural at Syracuse University. For Shahn it was perhaps his finest moment in a long and distinguished career.

It was also a great moment for Syracuse University, not only because of the historic event the mural depicts, but also because the University helped to highlight a great artist's moral statement. In sponsoring the mural, Syracuse did not encumber Shahn with committees, boards of review, or restrictions of any kind. He was allowed to choose the subject, the location, and the medium in which to work with no interference whatsoever. There appears to be nothing like the Syracuse mural at other academic institutions in the United States, and one must go to the University of Mexico to see Diego Rivera's work to find something comparable.

To most Americans the Sacco-Vanzetti case has become an obscure historical incident and few can remember the bitter controversy this so-called political murder caused in the 1920s. Initially the two anarchists had attracted attention to themselves with their radical strike activities and flight to Mexico in 1917 to evade the draft. Consequently law enforcement officials kept them under close surveillance after they returned to Massachusetts. When the paymaster of a shoe factory in South Braintree was held up and murdered on April 15, 1920, for a payroll of slightly more than $15,000, the police arrested Sacco and Vanzetti and charged them with the crime, although witnesses claimed they were miles away at the time. Despite such

9

IF IT HAD NOT BEEN FOR THESE THING, I MIGHT HAVE LIVE OUT MY LIFE TALKING AT STREET CORNERS TO SCORNING MEN. I MIGHT HAVE DIE, UNMARKED, UNKNOWN A FAILURE. NOW WE ARE NOT A FAILURE. THIS IS OUR CAREER AND OUR TRIUMPH. NEVER IN OUR FULL LIFE COULD WE HOPE TO DO SUCH WORK FOR TOLERANCE, FOR JOOSTICE, FOR MAN'S ONDERSTANDING OF MAN AS NOW WE DO BY ACCIDENT. OUR WORDS - OUR LIVES - OUR PAINS NOTHING! THE TAKING OF OUR LIVES - LIVES OF A GOOD SHOEMAKER AND A POOR FISH PEDDLER - ALL! THAT LAST MOMENT BELONGS TO US - THAT AGONY IS OUR TRIUMPH.

"Passion of Sacco and Vanzetti." 1958. Serigraph 25-3/4" x 17-1/2". Collection of Ben Shahn.

evidence, Webster Thayer, the presiding judge at the trial, made no secret of his contempt for the two Italian immigrants and allowed the prosecution to impress upon the jury the extent of the defendants' radical beliefs.

Trial irregularities and weaknesses in the case against them did not prevent a guilty verdict from being rendered and a death sentence from being passed. Although their lawyers worked for several years to obtain a new trial, claiming the first one had been unfair, all such motions were refused by Judge Thayer, who again sat at the rehearing seven years later. All chances of sparing their lives ended when Massachusetts Governor Alvan T. Fuller allowed the sentence to be carried out, basing his decision on his own investigation and the report of a committee headed by President A. Lawrence Lowell of Harvard University.

Fuller's refusal to act on a stay of execution for Sacco and Vanzetti touched off a renewed cry of injustice throughout the world. Rightly or wrongly, millions of people thought Sacco and Vanzetti had gone to the electric chair because of their anarchistic beliefs and not because they had been proven guilty of murder. Demonstrations erupted in England, France, Italy, Russia and Latin America, while intellectuals such as H. G. Wells, Edna St. Vincent Millay, Albert Einstein, Sinclair Lewis, and John Dos Passos took up their cause.

To some men it was more than a miscarriage of justice, it was a modern day crucifixion. Ben Shahn was one such man. He believed Sacco and Vanzetti were innocent and abhorred the apparent injustice of their trial. This was nothing new for Shahn,

Judge Webster Thayer as he appeared at the Courthouse in Dedham, Massachusetts. *United Press International.*

"Judge Webster Thayer." 1931-32. Gouache. Collection of Patricia M. Healy, New York, New York.

for even as a boy of eight in his native Russia he had already learned to hate injustice in any form. At the Hebrew school there he had heard a biblical story about an Ark that was being brought into the Temple, hauled by six white oxen, balanced on a single pole. The Lord knew the people would worry about the Ark falling off the pole, so to test their faith He gave orders that no one was to touch it, no matter what happened. One man saw it beginning to totter, and he rushed to help. He was struck dead. "I refused to go to school for a week after we read that story," he said. "It seemed so damned unfair. And it still does."

In the beginning, Shahn's involvement in the Sacco-Vanzetti case was more aesthetic than political or social. Not until he went to Europe in 1925, particularly in Paris, did he sense the ferment it had caused, not only among intellectuals, but also among the working classes. Children were being called Sacco and Vanzetti. Tugboats plying up and down the Seine River were named after the two alleged murderers. These things greatly impressed him. By the time Shahn returned to the United States, discontent over their fate had grown in this country and he actively became involved in the controversy.

"Even as a youngster," he said, "I always regretted not having lived in some great historic time; the time of Lincoln or Washington, or even during the Crucifixion. Then suddenly it came to me—this was a crucifixion itself—right in front of my eyes."

Shahn went to Boston twice to picket and each time he became more convinced of the injustice in the trial. He also thought he sensed a resentment in New England

against the success of foreigners who had prospered there, and this, he believed,
was why Sacco and Vanzetti were convicted. Earlier in the 1920s he had been appalled
by the so-called Palmer Raids aimed at radical immigrants throughout America. The
Attorney General of the United States, A. Mitchell Palmer, had harassed aliens with
mass arrests after World War I; men were often held for months without hearings
or trials, thousands of deportations followed, and so did many suicides.

These events had a marked influence on Shahn's work. Heretofore he had painted
in the Parisian School, but with some doubts and misgivings about himself. "Is this
the true me?" he wondered. "What do I share with Cézanne, who was a great master
being emulated by everyone?" Very little, he decided. Cézanne's father had been a
banker; Shahn's father was a cabinet maker and woodcarver. Cézanne had been sur-
rounded by ancient Roman ruins, but Shahn could only recall the last fire that burned
the Russian village he lived in as a boy. Shahn had a Talmudic education based
heavily on justice, while Cézanne, on the other hand, had been schooled in the Greek
and Roman classics. They had little in common.

Ben Shahn had indeed reached a crisis in his life. He had been told very early in art
school that you don't tell stories with paintings. Paintings had to have line, color,
and form. He felt that perhaps he was crippled in a certain way as a painter because
he also loved to tell stories with his paintings. Despite warnings from well-meaning
friends, Shahn made a decision. For better or worse he decided to tell stories,
especially of America, with an emphasis on social commentary and a deep sympathy
for mankind.

14

Demonstration for Sacco and Vanzetti on the Champs Elysee in Paris, France. *United Press International.*

"Demonstration in Paris." 1931-32. Gouache. 14-1/2" x 9-3/4".
Collection of Mr. and Mrs. Samuel Porter, Great Neck, New York.

The fate of Sacco and Vanzetti had haunted him ever since their execution. So in 1930 he started a series of 23 satirical gouache paintings based on the trial. His new work had a vigorous simplicity. It treated the connected events of the trial and the individuals involved in a manner reminiscent of the way Giotto recreated a religious drama, each complete in itself. This was a radical step for him, perhaps as radical as Ad Reinhart's black paintings appear to the public in the 1960s. Even though Shahn had never sold a painting for more than $50 at that time and no gallery wanted to exhibit his work, he felt that he had finally come of age as an artist. "This was now me," he said, "for better or worse, whether I was recognized or not, it did not bother me."

Shahn's idea for a mural based on the Sacco-Vanzetti theme originated during this same period when many struggling artists found themselves short of any visible means of support. Their plight had stirred the sympathies of many patrons and several committees were formed to devise helpful projects. In 1932 painters were invited to submit mural sketches by the old Museum of Modern Art for some possible but rather remote commissions.

Although ill at the time, Shahn submitted a huge panel he had just completed entitled: "The Passion of Sacco and Vanzetti." A few days later a prominent New Yorker invited him to dinner at his fashionable apartment in New York's East Sixties. After the other guests had departed and much to Shahn's surprise, the man offered the handsome price of $2,000 for his entry in the mural competition. Naturally Shahn was thrilled, that is, until the purchaser insisted on delivery before the exhibition

"The Lowell Committee." 1931-32. Gouache. 11″ x 15″. Collection of Patricia M. Healy, New York, New York.

"Bartolomeo Vanzetti and Nicola Sacco." 1931-32. Tempera. 10-1/2″ x 14-1/2″. Collection of The Museum of Modern Art, New York.

Bartolomeo Vanzetti (left) and Nicola Sacco (right) in the prisoners dock. *United Press International.*

"In the Courtroom Cage." 1931-32. Gouache. 11-1/2" x 14-1/2".
The Art Museum, Princeton University.

opened. Incensed at this blatant offer to forget his entry and withdraw it from competition, he walked all the way to his Brooklyn studio in a rage. That same night he found himself, in turn, threatened and cajoled, but he refused to withdraw.

This strange turn of events did bother him quite a bit, however, so he consulted educator Horace Kallen about it, because he too had been deeply involved in the Sacco-Vanzetti case during the trial. "You're not going to get that on the wall," Kallen told him. "You know you will never get anything else on the wall if you question this situation right now." Shahn knew it, but he did not care. "Well, then," said Kallen with a friendly laugh, "we will organize a Hang Shahn Committee."

Several articles in the New York newspapers hinted at trouble about Shahn's entry, but the full story was never published even though the opening of the exhibition was held up for two weeks. Shahn had won his battle. The 84 by 48 inch panel was exhibited and later sent on a national tour with other paintings. Until then he had thought of art as an individual thing; now he realized that a painting could have as great an impact as the written word. "This was my first skirmish against injustice via the paint brush," he said. "I was happy about it artistically, elated about it in spirit."

Somewhat ironically, Shahn had offered to sell the huge painting for $25 with the hope of avoiding the $2 taxi fare necessary to return it to his studio. Fortunately there were no purchasers until the Whitney Museum of American Art acquired it for its permanent collection in 1949.

Bartolomeo Vanzetti. 1931-32. Gouache. 14-1/2″ x 11-1/2″. Collection of Mrs. Edith Gregor Halpert, New York.

Shahn's Sacco-Vanzetti paintings were finally exhibited by Mrs. Edith Halpert at The Downtown Gallery, where they received a favorable reaction. In addition to the usual art public, the Sacco-Vanzetti theme created surprising interest among journalists and Italian immigrants who did not ordinarily visit art galleries. Almost overnight, as a result, Shahn attained artistic recognition and fame. His identification with the controversy, however, later prompted author Lincoln Kirstein to send him a book inscribed: "To Ben Shahn without whom this crime could never have been committed."

As the years passed, Shahn's stature in the art world continued to grow. His story-telling paintings stressed man's struggle with his surroundings and depicted in poetically realistic terms the life of workers on farms and in factories. Art critic James Thrall Soby summarized Shahn's contribution to contemporary art by noting that: "He is one of the most authentic and powerful of American humanists, an artist who translates the American scene into a strikingly personal statement of sympathy for mankind."

In 1947 The Museum of Modern Art gave him a retrospective of paintings, drawings, mural studies, and photographs, in which pictures such as "Death of a Miner" carried a message which seemed to ask: "Here is a tragedy. What is being done to prevent it from happening again?" A New York Times art critic wrote: "Often Shahn seems bent upon telling us that this is a terrible and cruel and a heart-breaking world. Yet there are the stimulating swift and keen imaginative flights. And his color can be such as an angel might use." To this Soby, director of the retrospective exhibi-

3,000 demonstrators (journeymen barbers) walk out in Brooklyn in a one-day strike to show their displeasure with the decision that Sacco and Vanzetti must die in the electric chair. *United Press International*

A group of pickets on the "Death Watch" in a detention room after being arrested in Boston. *United Press International.*

"Six Witnesses Who Bought Eels From Vanzetti." 1931-32. Watercolor. 10″ x 14-1/2″. Courtesy of Kennedy Galleries, Inc., New
York.

Frederick Katzman (left), the unrelenting prosecutor in the Sacco-Vanzetti trial, leaving the Boston State House with attorney Joseph Logan. *United Press International*.

tion, added: "In recent years Shahn has emerged as one of the most lyric of living American artists, his pictorial invention steadily more varied and rich, his technical fluency and warmth more and more impressive."

The Sacco-Vanzetti theme in Shahn's work quietly faded into obscurity until it was suddenly brought to light again in the autumn of 1965. Syracuse University had wanted him for some time to participate in its mural program. Therefore on October 25 of that year, I called on Shahn in an effort to persuade him to do a mural at the University. At 67 years of age, he no longer wanted to paint large canvasses. But as we talked for several hours, it became apparent that he might be willing to do a mosaic in the interior of one of our buildings, something that I readily agreed to.

Sensing that Syracuse was sincere in its promise to let him do any subject on any wall at the University, Shahn invited me to his studio.

Later he recalled that he really wanted to do public art because so many of his paintings had gone into private collections and were seldom seen. Therefore a mural at Syracuse University intrigued him, especially if it could be an interior mosaic. He walked over to the racks in the studio where many of his studies and pictures were stored and pulled out something he had done many years ago. I recognized it immediately as the old Sacco-Vanzetti theme with two additional panels I had never before seen.

27

"Sacco and Vanzetti and Their Guards." 1931-32. Gouache.
10" x 14-1/2". Collection of Patricia M. Healy, New York, New
York.

28 Shahn later confessed that he did this rather timidly because he thought: "My God! This is still a very controversial thing and becoming so again because of the many books and articles that are coming out on the subject." Apparently he was quite surprised to learn that this would be a suitable subject for a mural at Syracuse. Still he had his fingers crossed because the question of financing it had to be faced. "You won't be able to get the money for this subject," he said, "but perhaps I can help." He immediately called several wealthy friends to see if they might support our proposed project. Although I may have been optimistic about the possibilities of raising the money at first, these calls indicated few people would be willing to help because his friends quietly but firmly told him they could contribute nothing.

After this setback other possibilities were discussed, since the University's funds for this project were rather limited. Late that same afternoon Jacob Schulman's name was mentioned. Shahn told me Mr. Schulman was one of the more prominent collectors of his work, with a rather fine art collection based on Biblical themes by contemporary artists. Perhaps, Shahn suggested, Mr. Schulman would help. It was certainly worth a try so I decided to visit Mr. Schulman in Gloversville, New York, even before returning to Syracuse. At that moment Schulman had been searching around to find a suitable memorial to the son of Mr. and Mrs. Richard Evans II, his very dear and long-time friends. The Shahn mural interested him so he pledged his help. Had it not been for this cordial meeting and the strong support of the Schulmans, the Evanses and a number of other donors, this project probably would never have been completed.

Funeral hearse of Nicola Sacco and Bartolomeo Vanzetti leaving Massachusetts State Prison in Charleston after their execution. *United Press International.*

With financial backing assured, Shahn had to decide where to place the mural. He came to Syracuse University in December, 1965, to consider the possibilities. That visit took him into the interior of most of the buildings on campus because until then the mural had always been considered for an interior wall.

Shahn appeared pleased with the response he received as he searched for a suitable location and on one occasion he inquired about the building he was then looking at. When told it was the Ernest I. White Hall of the College of Law, a look of amazement suddenly came to his face. "You mean to tell me that Syracuse University would permit a mural by me based on the Sacco-Vanzetti theme in its Law School?" He was assured that this would be the case and the decision would be entirely up to him. At that moment the idea of a mosaic on the outside of one of Syracuse's buildings was born. Shahn asked whether this would be acceptable and once again the answer was yes. Therefore he began to look for an outside wall near the center of the University.

The east wall of the Huntington Beard Crouse Building appeared to be ideal for the theme he had selected. He chose this wall because of its position on campus, the heavy flow of student traffic that passed before it each day and the slight overhang of the building which would protect the mosaic during the winter. Although there were two gray doors on each end of the building, Shahn believed they could be utilized to good effect by placing a statement by Vanzetti on the narrow isolated sections beyond them. Thus the plan was complete.

"Staatliche Kunsthalle Baden-Baden." 1962. Poster. 33-3/4" x 24".
Collection of Ben Shahn.

Ben Shahn had done many murals during his career. In recent years he had also begun to do a number of mosaics and stained glass windows. These commissions introduced him to the work of Gabriel Loire of Chartres, France, one of the finest mosaic crafts- men in the world. He asked Loire to interpret his Sacco-Vanzetti theme for Syracuse University. When Loire agreed, Shahn went to Chartres to discuss the problems of interpretation, color and design, and work out the complex details needed to make it a success.

In September, 1966, Shahn wrote from France that "Loire, after thorough considera- tion of every detail involved in our project, gave an estimate of $27,000," or $8,000 more than the University originally expected to pay. The news created a good deal of apprehension because it appeared almost impossible to raise additional funds. Shahn told Loire this was a university undertaking and that Syracuse had gone to great lengths to achieve what he believed to be a monumental and historic work of art. Since Loire was eager to undertake the execution of the mosaic, he revised his estimate and reduced it to $25,000. There still remained Ben Shahn's fee, however, an estimated $10,000 to $15,000.

The mural project might have collapsed after all had it not been for Ben Shahn. He had begun to hold the mural in a very high scale of things he wanted to do, so he decided to make a substantial concession. "If it will make the difference between your ability to proceed or not to proceed with the work," he wrote, "I will make a gift to the University of my own charge for the designing and the various pieces of work that I have done in its preparation." At this point, Ben Shahn sacrificed all

Detail of the center section of the mural.

"The Passion of Sacco and Vanzetti." 1931-32. Gouache. 7-9/16"
x 15-9/16". Collection of Ben Shahn. Montage showing (from
left to right), a protest demonstration; Vanzetti (left), and Sacco
with Governor Fuller in the background; and the Lowell Committee at the anarchist's coffins, with Judge Webster Thayer at
the window of the Court House.

financial gain from the project. Even though he made two visits to Syracuse University and several trips to France to confer with Loire, he was not paid any money for these trips or for the Sacco-Vanzetti mural. With this kind of support from the Schulmans, the Evanses and from Shahn himself, the success of our work was assured.

Between September 1966 and June 1967, Gabriel Loire took charge of the actual assembly of the mural, working from Shahn's design. Loire used a variety of materials to reduce the glare that is inevitable in mosaic work. Tiny pieces of marble and glass, often with a surface of less than an inch, were secured on the 48 inch by 72 inch epoxy fibre boards so the mural could be shipped to Syracuse in sections where it could then be bolted to lattice work on the wall.

Mr. Antonio DiValentin, the individual responsible for completing the mural in Syracuse, brought it to the University late in the summer of 1967. This was not the first Shahn work DiValentin had finished for Loire so he proceeded to place the many separate slabs of the mosaic on the wall with amazing speed. Then be began the long and tedious job of making it a unified work of art by sealing the seams and filling in the cracks between the sections. To most observers DiValentin's competence was obvious, for it is impossible to find the original seams everyone had seen when the mural was first erected on the wall.

The completed work stands as an imposing example of contemporary art and most critics who have seen it feel that it might well be one of Ben Shahn's greatest works.

Detail of Bartolomeo Vanzetti and Nicola Sacco from the original cartoon of the mural.

38 The mural is divided into three parts, with a central panel and two flanking sections. The central portion shows the two men handcuffed together. On the left are the rioters who protested against the execution, while to the right the Lowell Committee stands over the coffins of Sacco and Vanzetti, with Judge Webster Thayer in the courthouse window behind them.

Two narrow sections on each end of the building contain a moving statement by Bartolomeo Vanzetti taken from a letter to his son:

> "If it had not been for these thing, I might have live out my life talking at street corners to scorning men. I might have die, unmarked, unknown, a failure. Now we are not a failure. This is our career and our triumph. Never in our full life could we hope to do such work for tolerance, for joostice, for man's onderstanding of man as now we do by accident. Our words—our lives—our pains—nothing! The taking of our lives—lives of a good shoemaker and a poor fish-peddler—all! That last moment belongs to us—that agony is our triumph."

Shahn has told the Sacco-Vanzetti story simply and well. There is no explosive hatred in the mural. Rather it exhibits great compassion combined with irony and anger and relies heavily on moral values. There is also a great deal of symbolism in the work, to be sure, for Sacco's shadow falls upon the cold, gray courthouse to indicate that a smear on justice has been made by this poorly handled trial. The original version has been changed slightly to increase the feeling of loneliness that one senses in standing before it. In the earlier interpretation, first exhibited at The Museum of Modern Art, Shahn had been given an arbitrary space in which to work. He had more

Detail of the mural showing the Lowell Committee: Robert Grant (left), President A. Lawrence Lowell of Harvard University (center), and President Samuel W. Stratton of M.I.T.

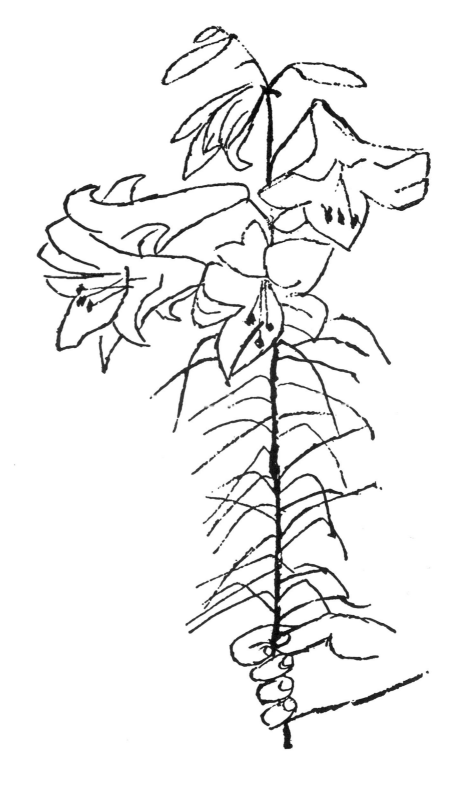

room at Syracuse. He believes the whole design is infinitely greater as a result, and better than the original work.

Since Shahn considered Vanzetti the most important individual involved, he made Vanzetti's figure larger than that of Sacco in much the same way Medieval artists characterized important figures of that time.

When Shahn first saw the culmination of the work he had begun in the early 1930s, he was elated. "I feel as a composer must feel who had written it all out, you know, and never had it played before. Now, I have finally had the good fortune to see the performance by Mr. Loire and it is absolutely perfect."

For Ben Shahn, the mural completed a dream that started 35 years ago with a series of paintings in which he first found himself as an artist. Since then he has become noted for his independence of thought in emphasizing that man must work from his heart if he hopes to achieve equality, understanding, and justice in this world.

Detail of the mural showing demonstrators.

44

"Judge Webster Thayer." 1931-32. Gouache. 14-1/2" x 9-3/4".
Collection of Philip Wittenberg, New York.

"Demonstration in Union Square, New York." 1931-32. Watercolor. 14-1/2" x 10". Collection of Ben Shahn.

Detail from the mural of Massachusetts Governor Alvan T. Fuller, who appointed a three-man Advisory Committee to review the case.

Detail of Governor Alvan T. Fuller from the original cartoon of the mural.

NERS TO SCORN
ING MEN.
I MIGHT HAVE
DIE UNMARKED,
UNKNOWN A FAIL
URE. NOW WE
ARE NOT A FAIL
URE. THIS IS OUR
CAREER AND OUR
TRIUMPH.
NEVER IN OUR
FULL LIFE COULD
WE HOPE TO DO
SUCH WORK FOR

AMERICAN PAINTING AT MID-CENTURY: AN UNORTHODOX VIEW
BY BEN SHAHN

My point of view is not that of either historian or expert, but of participant. As such, it will no doubt be myopic, biased, personal, prejudiced, slanted—I am anticipating probable comment—

Whatever accuracy I can predict for my remarks will be accuracy as to the mood of people, particularly artists; what things stirred among us; the level of controversy at certain times; the degree to which public events found their expression in art.

These things I can recount with the sharp accuracy of one who has never achieved the detached, serene outlook of the bystander—who has a penchant for turning up in the target area in both artistic and civil affairs.

My first discontent with art—by no means my last—arose during the mid-twenties. I began to be aware, then, that my pieces and those of my contemporaries were continually a re-statement of the product of earlier artists; that much of their work was, in its turn, a reiteration of what had gone before.

I'm quite sure that my initial rebellion came from boredom and impatience with pre-digested food, rather than of any clear convictions about the role and function of art.

"Self Portrait." 1955. Brush and ink. 9 3/4" x 6-1/8". Collection of The Museum of Modern Art, New York.

We painted the "Nu Couche," the "Femme Assise," the "Nature Morte," the "Bagneuse," the "Paysage," the "Fete Champetre," ad nauseum. We elaborated, over acres of canvas, those observations, and subjects that were considered the particular, special, precious stuff of art.

I shared the conviction of most young artists that new soil would surely provide me with a new outlook. And, lured by Delacroix's remarkable notebooks, I made my own particular pilgrimage to Africa. There, devoutly, I saw through the eyes of Delacroix.

I am recounting this bit of personal history only because it may serve to reveal a certain nostalgia the young artist has to belong somewhere or to something. Art in America during the twenties was an isolated activity, alien to the common life—a pursuit of long-haired and immoral foreigners.

Surfeited with Delacroix I journeyed to Paris where I saw through the eyes, successively, of Matisse, Rouault, Soutine and Picasso. I hadn't yet acquired the temerity to use my own.

Europe was at that time a maelstrom of modes, "isms," and genuine search—and who was to separate the grain from the chaff? Political "isms" were wedded to artistic ones in some of the most incredible misalliances of history. Surrealism, bedded with Communism, announced their union through Breton's Surrealist Manifesto. Futurism in Italy leaned tenderly on the arm of the Fascists. Constructivism still enjoyed the favors of the Bolshevists in Russia. Every political view, every *Weltanschauung*, had

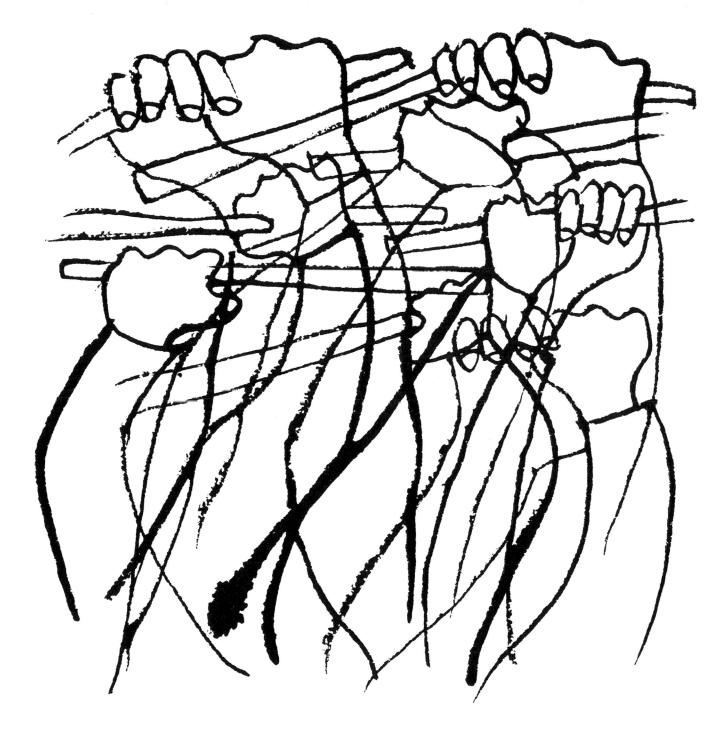

The line drawings in this book are in the Collection of Ben Shahn.

52 its counterpart in art. Every imaginative flight of artists must be rationalized by attenuated philosophical argument.

I was greatly affected by *L'Esprit Nouveau,* impressed by the pavillion of its editors, Ozenfant and Le Corbusier in the Exposition. I attended the lectures of Leonce Rosenberg on Cubism. I argued art and politics—as everyone did. Political views then often incurred high feeling, but not ostracism. I marched with the *"Confeder-acion,"* as was proper.

Back in America in 1929 I saw the many currents of Europe reflected "as in a mirror, darkly." Matisse, so full of verve in Paris, seemed a little illogical here. His idiom was without roots in our culture and it languished like a hot-house plant. Still we nursed it, as we nursed the vivid forms of Picasso and the lush nudes of Renoir. Each of the noted French innovators had his little knot of argumentative disciples here, divided artistically, but united in the great crusade against Babbitt. And it is only with some hindsight that one can appraise the extent of that folly.

The great event known as the *Crash* wasn't really much of an event for the artist, except inasmuch as it led him on to new things. As John Sloan said in 1933, "Artists have always been in a depression. It's just that other people have joined us now." Most of us, who had just managed to glean a living here or there, while we devoted our chief interest to art, had now, as someone said, "to devote ourselves to the problems of color, line, form, food and shelter."

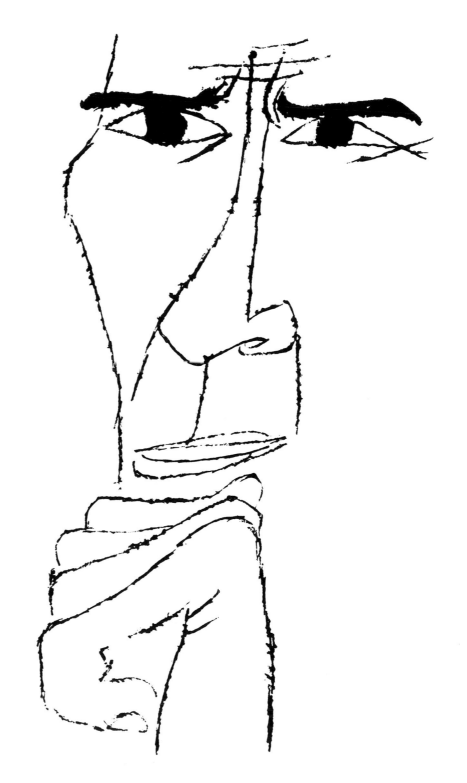

53

54   But Sloan's comment was, in truth, the key to a new time. The artist was joined in his customary poverty by almost the whole population. Seemingly fixed barriers melted away, and what I, and a scattering of others, consider a tremendously important period in our history began to take shape.

As the artists' never-very-visible means of support dwindled, the sympathies of patrons were stirred, and a number of committees were formed to devise helpful projects. One of the first of these was undertaken by The Museum of Modern Art. Painters were invited to submit mural sketches and details toward the objective of several rather vaguely described, possible commissions.

My own submission was now no Paris-inspired achievement of pure form. It was a huge panel, taken from a series of paintings that I had just completed dealing with the deaths of Sacco and Vanzetti. This was my first skirmish against injustice via the paint brush. I was happy about it artistically, elated about it in spirit.

The picture was not warmly received by the Museum. It so distressed that great and admirable Institution that I found myself, in turn, threatened, cajoled, persuaded, and finally, in a delicately roundabout way, offered a handsome price for the painting, if only I would forget my invitation and withdraw it. It is only fair to mention that it was not withdrawn and was reproduced in the catalog.

That provided me with the stunning realization that patronage is not always pure.

56 It provided me, also, with a set of contradictions that must always plague the path of the artist, and that I shall be happy to pass on to you; first, that patronage may want something of art beyond the mere pleasure of looking at it; second, that, while the artist's worth revolves about his being independent, original, creative, entirely his own man—patronage is quite likely to shun him, on just those grounds. And then conversely, the artist who is imitative, not too scrupulous about lifting, an habitue of bandwagons, may enjoy the favors of patronage—on just those grounds.

Patronage, which involves the spending of money, usually likes to be safe, as well as discriminating. It often feels safest in the buying of art that resembles something important that it has seen somewhere before. Of course patronage ought, ideally, to understand its relation to art. One would like to think of patronage as a means whereby the great images of an era, the essential comments upon that era, may be preserved and carried on into tradition. Realistically, it may indicate anything from a flair for fads, or an instance of vanity, to a most discerning vision and high purpose. Every artist must decide, whether he will resist trends in patronage that, at one point or another, may become outright demands; whether he is convinced that there is sufficient solid value in what he has to express to warrant jeopardizing his livelihood.

And to complicate the contradictions—there is the passionate desire of the artist to bring new vision to others, and new understanding. He will be eager for some sign of recognition, of response to his efforts. Patronage is the most tangible form of response.

58 For me, as for other artists in the early thirties, these problems became highly academic. Patronage bowed out.

The American public today is wont to look askance at the Roosevelt pump-priming measures. Our national stomach prefers to forget its hunger pangs of the early thirties. Repudiation of our recent greatness is in the air—as is repudiation of the art, theatre, music, writing, and great public welfare projects that were undertaken. Nevertheless, the cultural pump-priming of that time begot an enlightened public for art today. It begot, too, the first widespread indigenous art movement that the country has known.

In its numerous art projects the Government, with incomparable restraint, accepted all attitudes in art, all schools and all points of view. Abstract paintings stood against PWA walls alongside works of extreme leftist content. Still-lifes favoring Cézanne shared space with still-lifes in the National Academy tradition. The works of the great lined up democratically with those of the unknown. Mural sketches were judged with no names attached. The only standard brought to bear upon the indigent artist was simply whether he was an artist.

Thus the change wrought by government-supported art projects was mainly quantitative. In quality the average, through sheer weight of numbers, had to be low. The quantitative aspect alone, however, served art well. It provided an un-judged, uncensored fellowship to hundreds of artists who are many of them, even now, just coming into maturity. It discovered a number of talents that have already moved to

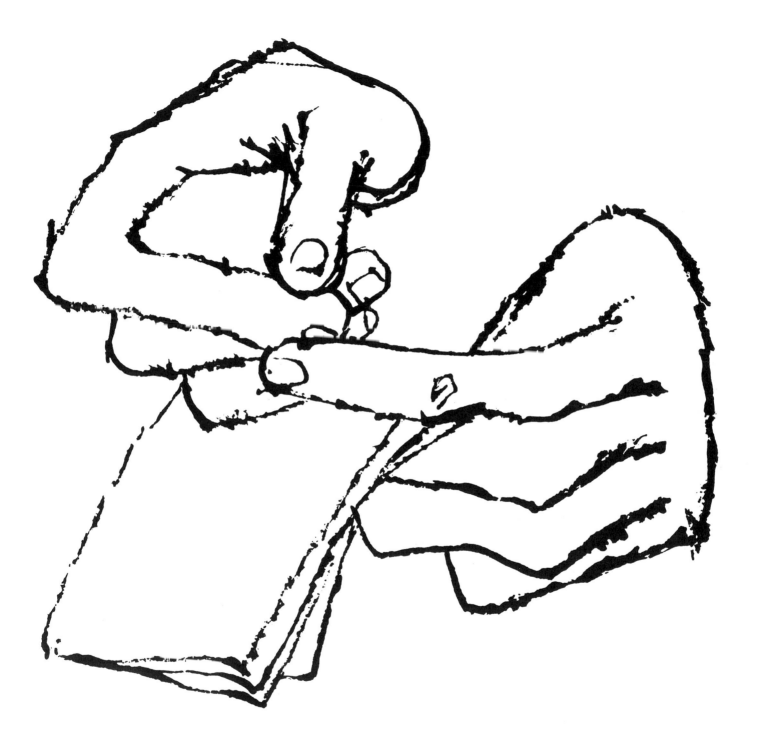

first place in art—and that otherwise in all probability might never have emerged at all. Jacob Lawrence and Jack Levine are among these. And there are dozens of others whose work has given American art distinction and honor throughout the world.

Content-wise, the art projects worked an interesting if less universal change. The artist, no longer hygienically sealed from the ordinary public, surveyed it with interest, and found in it an inexhaustible source of art motifs. Of course the distinguishing characteristic of project art was its pluralism. There was great exploration of form, as there was of techniques. There were even extensive projects analyzing the artists' materials. But people, and the general condition, formed the new, and perhaps predominant element. And as a result, we have, for better or for worse, a heritage of depression symbolism exceeding that of any other phase of our existence—if one excepts advertising.

The once-empty Utrillo-inspired street, brought home from abroad, was now wont to contain an eviction scene, or the bankruptcy signs which, in those days, stared from every third window. The relief station, the breadline, the unemployed in all their sorrows comprised the new imagery. "Ecce Homo" was the forgotten man. Dust storms, desperate migrations, and the burning of western wheat found their way into art as middle-class prosperity had never done. And, as in all other times, there was the art that was warmly felt and genuine, and there was the spurious and the imitative stepping along close on its heels.

On the more optimistic side, giant new government projects—dams, parks, high-
ways, playgrounds, constituted material for landscapes—and it was sometimes
inventively handled. Labor gained a now place in the sun in government, a place of
eminence in art. The American past was spread before the citizenry across the walls
of post-offices, railway stations, hospitals, schools and other public buildings from
coast to coast. The teaching of art, both to children and adults, was a country-
wide enterprise.

With the advent of war, the curtain fell upon art, except in those few instances in
which it could contribute to the war effort. When it arose again in 1945 and 1946,
the art landscape was well-nigh unrecognizable.

Government interest in art had melted away. Completely forgotten, within those
few war years, was the earmarking of one percent of the appropriation for any federal
building for mural and sculpture decoration. What had seemed to be a growing recognition of the desirability of a cabinet post to cover education and the arts, had now
vanished. There was no government art activity of any kind, but there was prosperity,
there was patronage, and there was greater general interest in art than ever before.

The Whitney opening of 1946 revealed an overwhelming tide toward abstract art.
One critic commented, "The Whitney Annual is a sedimentary deposit of mind
beneath the explosions of modern living. One may rummage among the abstrac-
tionists of 1946 to discover only the outlook of the generation before the first
world war."

What had become of the polyglot human procession that had crowded over the canvasses of the thirties? Had they marched on into an art limbo (where perhaps a good many of them belonged) and taken their authors along? Did this opening reveal an entirely new generation in art? Names in the corners of canvasses—and only that, betrayed the fact that here was just the same small art fraternity that had exhibited at the Whitney for the past decade or so.

I shall now unabashedly align the change in the art landscape with the change in political atmosphere—with its sidelights on criticism and patronage. Repudiation was indeed in the air. The Congress was busily vanquishing the ghost of the New Deal, and the Reign of Committees had begun. Relations between the recent allies, the United States and Russia, chilled, provoked by mutual intransigeance. Liberalism was in bad odor, both for its New Deal leanings, and for its indulgence of Communism. Suspicion, accusation and renunciation grew.

In this rather delicate atmosphere, the State Department, with the advice of experts, bought a number of paintings, the work of artists whom the experts considered "top-flight." The collection had been requested by members of our diplomatic service, who wished to exhibit American paintings that would improve our cultural standing abroad.

The pictures were stopped in mid-journey, hastily withdrawn from the tour and returned to the United States. Hearst's newspapers had launched an attack upon them, in the course of which, more space must have been allotted to art than ever

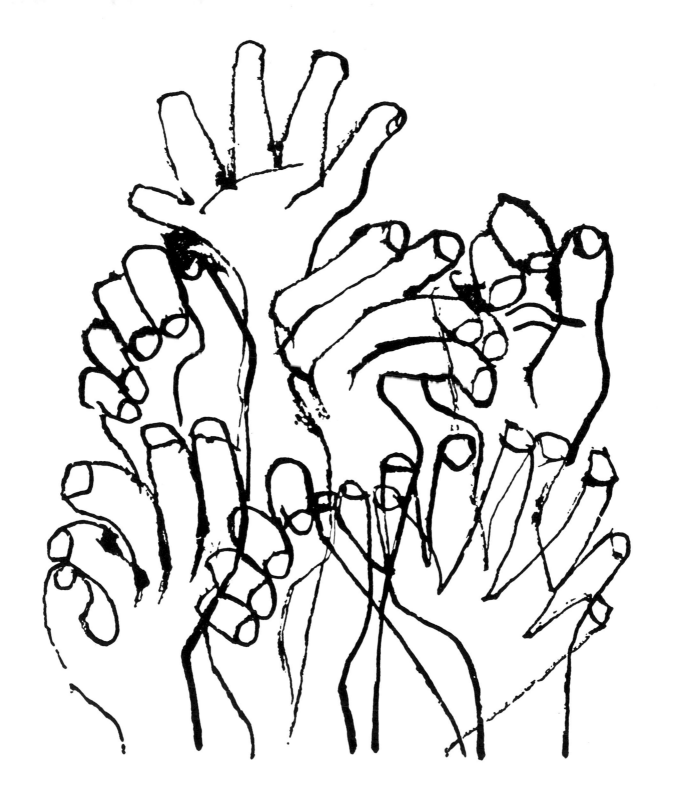

before in the history of those papers. *Look* magazine, too, and I think with the best of intentions, had carried a number of reproductions of the paintings, in pretty inaccurate color, with some such caption as "Look What your Taxes Are Buying."

Thus called to the attention of Congress, the pictures failed to conform to any of the Solons' ideas about what art ought to be. The ensuing hullabaloo forced then Secretary of State Marshall to cancel the exhibition. The paintings were quietly sold to museums and collectors under sealed bids.

A sharp realization of the changed time was brought home to me personally at the time of my 1949 show at The Downtown Gallery in New York. Henry McBride, who had had many kind words to say about my painting in the past, now professed to see, in an allegorical red beast that I had done, some sort of Communistic symbolism. The beast, in truth, represented a Chicago tenement fire. Mr. McBride suggested deportation for me.

And soon thereafter artists were subjected to a new variety of hazing. Congressman Dondero, of Michigan, in a series of speeches on the floor of the House, attributed to all modern art a plot to undermine Democracy and substitute Communism. He described artists in such tender terms as "germ-carrying art vermin," "subversives," "human art termites," "international art thugs," "art with political murder" (that one was for me) and "the role of infamy." He spread the names of individual artists over the pages of the Congressional Record! Coupled with misinformed statements against which there was no redress.

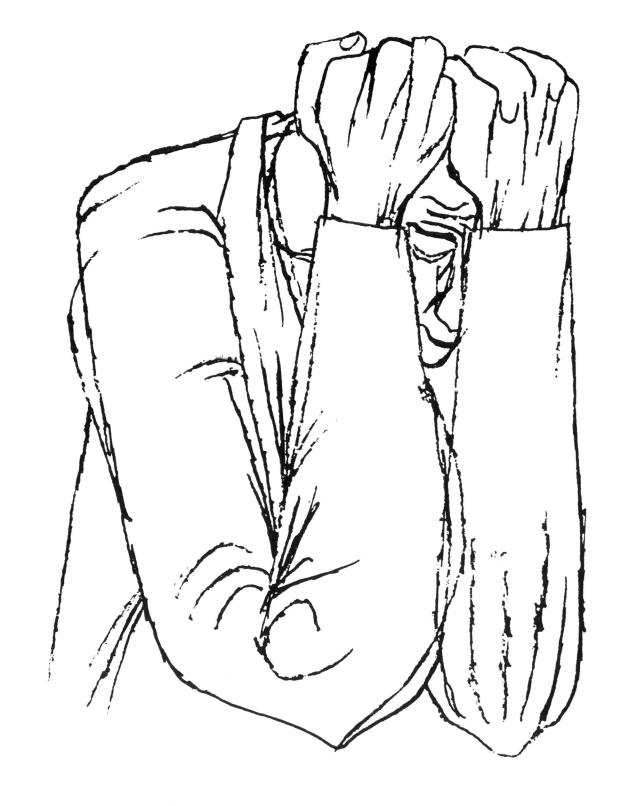

65

Mr. Dondero's remarks were not without precedent. They fairly duplicated, epithet for epithet, an abusive essay against modern art that had appeared some months earlier in the Soviet publication, Voks Bulletin. The Soviet writer, Vladimir Kamenev, it appears, would forcibly protect glorious Russian art against modern forms, as Mr. Dondero would protect "our glorious American art" from being stabbed in the back.

Having further recommended that art organizations adopt allegiance measures and that newspapers exercise supervision over their critics, the Congressman went on to say: "Of course this simple statement, made with kindly intent, was immediately seized upon and distorted. . . ."

And lest all this amuse you, let me add that Emily Genauer, forthright and independent critic of the *World Telegram*, courageously challenged the statements; then promptly lost her job.

Museums also were not spared in the Dondero crusade. Scurrilous names applied to the directors of several museums were such as to have earned the kindly Congressman libel suits, had he not been safely entrenched within his congressional immunity.

And, as a poignant little aside, let's note here that it was at about this time that T. S. Eliot became spokesman for pretentious philosophy of the elite that offered comforting asylum, and emotional haven to so many refugees from the facts of life.

Without mentioning the Dondero affair, The Museum of Modern Art, Boston's Institute of Contemporary Art, and the Whitney Museum issued a joint statement affirming their policies with regard to modern art. The statement was dignified, decent, and liberal, and might happily serve as a model for the conduct of any art institution in a Democracy.

That it was a little suspect on all sides is, I think, an enlightening clue to our times. Many advanced artists regarded the statement as a timid retreat toward conventional art. Conservative artists thought the statement pink-tinged. Some leftists thought it a betrayal of the artists' best interest.

Thus the art controversies which in the twenties and thirties would have been on the level of polemics—however acrimonious—now had new elements injected into them: suspicion, accusation, and fear of attainder. Artists, perhaps for the first time in history, were visited by government agents, quizzed at length about their friends, their associations, their activities. You may disagree with me that such a political atmosphere can have any effect upon the esthetic content of art, to stimulate the trend toward abstraction, or toward anything else. I believe that it has. Abstract painting is, politically speaking, about the most non-committal statement that can be made in art. True. Mr. Dondero did his utmost to attach subversiveness to it. But he was mistaken in this, as in so many other matters. Abstract art had left its political banners far behind and has for many years gone its way, "disengaged."

I do not mean, by this, to undervalue abstract art as such. An impressive segment of abstract work is unquestionably of the most genuine conviction. Anyone knowing the past work of Stuart Davis or a number of other abstract painters—or of such superlative sculptors as Noguchi, David Smith or Alex Calder, could never doubt their intense belief (indeed realization) of the ultimate validity of that form of expression.

But fashions in art, of whatever complexion, are merely the camp-followers of authentic art. The exaggerated scenes of violence of the thirties aped the thoughtful work of that time. So do the repetitive abstractions of today, wherein the hands are the hands of the artist but the voice is the voice of Baroness Rebaye.

A further influence, without which we cannot properly assess the present meanings of art, is that of criticism. There are scores of artists who are unable to subsist on the proceeds of painting alone—I suppose that really constitutes the majority. For them criticism takes the place of patronage. It affirms, or it dismisses. Too often capriciously, it doles out the coveted adjectives; three, two, one to a name. And that is the artist's small acknowledgment for his pains. So it is hardly surprising that many artists, especially young ones, seek their artistic pastures where the adjectives grow thickest.

There is a considerable body of very responsible criticism today that appears to me to deserve a high place among all critical writings. I feel that James Soby has broadened the general scope of art understanding greatly. There are Robert Coates of *The New Yorker*, Tom Hess of *Art News*, Jean Charlot, who, besides being an artist is one of the most penetrating of art writers. There is Aline Louchheim of the *Times*,

whose recent piece on Jacob Lawrence won instant recognition for a new and valuable orientation toward art. There are many other critics who deserve being read, because their view of art is within a world perspective and neither magnifies nor distorts what it sees.

Then there are current among critics several varieties of astigmatism that exercise a quasi-religious sort of tyranny over artists and public.

Not long ago I stood with a friend looking at a painting of Edward Hopper's. My friend remarked: "I admire Hopper. It takes courage to paint like that, these days."

The reason why it takes courage is because of the pervasiveness of such critical gems as the following: "The representative element in a work of art may or may not be harmful, but it is always irrelevant. For to appreciate a work of art, we must bring with us nothing from life, no knowledge of its affairs and ideas, no familiarity with its emotions."

The above sentences were those of Clive Bell, an early prophet of the present tide. One wonders on reading them, why it is that art which must have no content, needs to lean upon writing that is so painfully expository. Now let me read a few lines from a modern prophet:

"The message of modern art . . . it is precisely that means are content. Pigment and its abstract combinations on canvass . . matter, colors, and the surfaces on which they are placed, are as important as ideas. . . . All existence is sanctified."

That is from Clement Greenberg, critic for the *Partisan Review*. Mr. Greenberg is a leading Apostle of that sort of painting which negates human meaning. But when the implications of such a denial of man touch him personally, he then suddenly understands. Witness his outcry against the award of the Bollingen Prize to Ezra Pound, an award which he felt gave acceptance to Pound's anti-Semitism. Here are Mr. Greenberg's words:

"In any case," he says, "I am sick of the art adoration that prevails among cultured people, more in our time than in any other: that art stillness which condones almost any moral or intellectual failing on the artist's part as long as he seems a successful artist. It is still justifiable to demand that he be a successful human being before anything else, even if at the cost of his art. As it is, psychopathy has become endemic among artists and writers in whose company the moral idiot is tolerated as perhaps nowhere else in society."

One wishes that Mr. Greenberg might extend his lucidity to the field of panting, and that he might extend his racial indignation to include the entire human race. For the annulment of human content and human importance is a necessary concomitant of an atomic age. And an art that subscribes to that is, as our critic suggests, an art of moral idiocy.

That brings us to a consideration of what may lie ahead for art.

Perhaps it is presumptuous for an artist to make predictions as to the future of art. I believe that its course will be determined by the moods of society, by political situations, by kinds of patronage, and so on. If art must revolve about an elite, it may become increasingly abstruse—although that's merely a guess. We have witnessed the banalities that the totalitarian condition produces. And there is no tangible evidence that Democracy will necessarily yield a good art. What then, can be said to be a favorable condition for art?

Looking backward, one might observe that the surpassingly beautiful art of the past has emerged from those periods when man was deeply stirred spiritually, or by great ideas. That was true of the Golden Age of Greece, whose intellectual and emotional concepts we still own. Again, during the Renaissance, artists and poets were captured by the refinements of religious devotion. We carry its images about with us now, and are the better for it.

The last half of the nineteenth century in France—in all of Europe—saw the rise of the free and sovereign individual. His human-ness was his paramount quality; and that included his moralities and his immoralities, his inner visions and his outer grossness, all of which were celebrated in the arts of the time. Whatever pretentions to cosmic authority may have been made by the art of the "isms," it succeeded only in being the more human.

I doubt that what now seems to be an atomic age, or is in any case a sort of scientifico-mechanical age, will ever be greatly distinguished for its contributions to the human spirit. But perhaps later generations, if there are to be later generations, will discover in it qualities which the near view prevents one's seeing.

74   It is claimed that non-objective art is the perfect expression of such an age, and perhaps it is true. For the non-objective painting claims validity only for its mechanics; for the materials with which it is made and the manner of their organization. It rejects man, his life, his visions, his philosophies, his future. It is even affirmative in the sense that it asks us to be of good cheer; the machine can absorb our emotions and contain our soul.

Still, I believe that the increasing interest and activity in art is in essence rebellion against absolutism of science and mechanics; that it evidences a widespread nostalgia for the human touch and for the personal statement.

For so much that we live with an experience today has become devoid of personality. Objects that we handle and use are mass-produced, our clothing, mass-designed. Our entertainment, in great part, must needs be reduced to common denominators and cliches. Mass-communication has stereotyped public information, and with that the personal truth-gathering, the truth-telling that we have held so essential to our well-being. Even opinion must be processed editorially before it may be relayed to the ordinary citizen.

But art is still the citadel of the individual. It is one of the few remaining outposts of free speech—unprocessed speech. The personal touch of the artist's hand remains ineradicably upon his canvas. Whatever he says or feels is communicated directly and without modification to those who look at his work.

But I think that artists ought to recognize this, that there is no moral reason why art ought to go on if it has nothing further to express. Nor is there any moral or aesthetic reason why the public ought to bend the knee in reverence before the mere fact of art. We might assume instead that art is important only if it essays to be important.

If it adopts the manners and outlook and philosophy of a minor expression, then a minor expression it will be. If it aspires to be aesthetic of double-talk, just that will be its position, nothing more; and life will walk around it and let it alone.

Society needs more than anything else to be reminded that man is, in himself, ultimate value. It needs to be reminded that neither the pressure of events nor the exigencies of diplomacy can warrant the final debasement of man. We need a resurgence of the humanities, a rebirth of spirit. Art, because it is the innate expression of man, speaks also in final values, tends to reaffirm the individual. Art is neither use, nor appointed task. But given human compulsions, some intellectual stature and great competence, it can perhaps bring man back into focus as being of supreme importance, in which case it will have earned an honored place among the humanities.

Ben Shahn

April   1951

Ben Shahn

SELECTED BIBLIOGRAPHY

WRITINGS AND STATEMENTS BY SHAHN

"An Artist's Credo." *College Art Journal.* (Autumn, 1949), 43-45. (Condensation of paper read at the Second Annual Art Conference, Woodstock, New York, August 28-29, 1948.)

"Artists in Colleges." *The Christian Scholar.* (Summer, 1960), 97-113.

"Aspects of the Art of Paul Klee." *Museum of Modern Art Bulletin.* (Summer, 1950), 6-9. (Speech delivered at the first of a series of symposia presented by the Junior Council of the Museum of Modern Art, New York.)

"Bill." *The Visual Craft of William Golden.* Cipe Pineles Golden, Kurt Weihs, Robert Stunsky (eds.). New York: George Braziller, 1962, 126-127. (Includes reproductions of work Shahn has done for the Columbia Broadcasting System.)

Brandon, Henry ". . . A Conversation with Ben Shahn." *New Republic.* (July 7, 1958), 15-18. (A taped conversation for the *Sunday Times,* London, which appeared in the March 16, 1958, issue of that newspaper.)

"How an Artist Looks at Aesthetics." *Journal of Aesthetics and Art Criticism.* (September, 1954), 46-51. (Paper presented at the annual meeting of the American Society for Aesthetics, East Lansing, Michigan, November 20, 1953.)

"In Defense of Chaos." *The Collected Prints of Ben Shahn.* Kneeland McNulty (ed.). Philadelphia: Philadelphia Museum of Art, 1967, 13-16. (Paper presented at the International Design Conference in Aspen, Colorado, 1966.)

"In the Mail: Art versus Camera." *The New York Times.* (February 13, 1955), Section 2, 15. (A letter to the editor in which Shahn takes exception to the review by Aline B. Saarinen, "The Camera versus the Artist," which discusses the photographic exhibition "The Family of Man" organized by Edward Steichen.)

"In Homage." in "The Talk of the Town." *The New Yorker.* (September 29, 1962), 31-33. (Interview with Shahn on the memorial dedicated to President Franklin D. Roosevelt, June 2, 1962, in Roosevelt, New Jersey.)

Miller, Dorothy C. and Barr, Alfred H. Jr. (eds.). *American Realists and Magic Realists.* New York: The Museum of Modern Art, 1943. (Catalogue of exhibition, statement by Shahn, 52-53.)

Morse, John D. "Ben Shahn: An Interview." *Magazine of Art.* (April, 1944), 136-141.

Morse, John D. "Henri Cartier-Bresson." *Magazine of Art.* (May, 1947), 189. (Shahn's opinions on the photographer and on photography in general.)

Paragraphs on Art. New York: The Spiral Press, 1952. ("The second in a series of a brief personal credos prepared at the request of The Spiral Press. These Paragraphs by Ben Shahn gathered from speeches made at various times and places over the past few years. . . .")

"Photos for Art." *U. S. Camera.* (May, 1946), 57.

"Realism Reconsidered." *Perspecta.* (1957), 28-35. (Text of talk given before the Institute of Contemporary Art, London, February, 1956, in connection with the Tate Gallery's exhibition, "Modern Art in the United States.")

Rodman, Selden (ed.). "Ben Shahn Speaking." *Perspectives USA.* (January, 1952), 59-72.

Rodman, Selden. *Conversations with Artists.* New York: Devin-Adair Co., 1957. (Interview with Shahn, 189-193, 221-228.)

"Shahn in Amsterdam." *Art in America.* (No. 3, 1961), 62-67. (Shahn presents and interprets a wide selection of his paintings.)

"Symposium: The Relation of Painting and Sculpture to Architecture." *Interiors.* (May, 1951), 102.

"The Artist and the Politicians." *Art News.* (September, 1953), 34-35, 67.

"The Artist's Point of View." *Magazine of Art.* (November, 1949), 266, 269. (Paper presented at the Seventh Annual Conference on Art Education sponsored by the Museum of Modern Art, New York, March 18-20, 1949. Balcomb Greene, Robert Motherwell, and Shahn participated in the session, "The Artist's Point of View.")

The Biography of a Painting. New York: Paragraphic Books; and Fitz Henry and Whiteside, Ltd., Canada, 1966.

The Biography of a Painting. Cambridge: Harvard University, Fogg Museum, 1956. (Fogg Picture Books, No. 6.)

". . . The Future of the Creative Arts: A Symposium . . .," *University of Buffalo Studies.* (February, 1952), 125-128. (One of several symposia on the theme "The Outlook for Mankind in the Next Half-Century," at the Niagara Frontier Convocation, December 7-8, 1951. (Includes text by Shahn; remarks reprinted in Alfred H. Barr, Jr. (ed.). *Masters of Modern Art.* New York: The Museum of Modern Art, 1954, 162)

The Shape of Content. Cambridge: Harvard University Press, 1957. (The Charles Eliot Norton lectures of 1956-1957. Reprinted New York, 1960, as Vintage Book V-108.)

"They Can Rank with the Greatest Works of Art, But . . . Famous Painter Asks: Are Cartoons Now Among the Obits?" *Art News.* (October, 1954), 50.

"What is Realism in Art?" *Look.* (January 13, 1953) , 44-45.

BOOKS ILLUSTRATED BY SHAHN

Aleichem, Sholom. *Inside Kasrilevke.* New York: Schocken Books, 1965.

Berry, Wendell. *November Twenty Six Nineteen Hundred Sixty Three.* New York: George Braziller, 1964.

Berryman, John. *Hommage to Mistress Bradstreet.* New York: Farrar, Straus & Cudahy, 1956.

Dahlberg, Edward. *The Sorrows of Priapus.* Norfolk, Connecticut: New Directions Books, 1957.

Hudson, Richard, and Shahn, Ben. *Kuboyama and the Saga of the Lucky Dragon.* New York and London: Thomas Yoseloff, 1965.

Ish-Kishor. *A Boy of Old Prague.* New York: Pantheon Books, 1963.

Owen, Wilfred. *Thirteen Poems.* Northampton, Massachusetts: Gehenna Press, 1956.

Reid, Alastair. *Once Dice Trice.* Boston and Toronto: Little, Brown & Co., 1958.

Roth, Cecil. *Haggadah for Passover.* Paris: Trianon Press, 1966. (Translation, introduction and notes by Roth, copied and illustrated by Shahn.)

Samstag, Nicholas. *Kay-Kay Comes Home. A Fable of Enthusiasm.* New York: Curt Valentin, 1962.

Shahn, Ben. *Ecclesiastes.* Paris: Trianon Press, 1967. (Handwritten and illustrated by Shahn.)

Shahn, Ben. *Ecclesiastes* or, *The Preacher.* New York: Spiral Press, 1965. (In the King James translation of the Bible, engraved in wood by Stefan Martin, with calligraphy by David Soshensky.)

Shahn, Ben. *Love and Joy About Letters.* New York: Grossman Publishers; Toronto: The Musson Book Company, 1963.

Shahn, Ben. *Maximus of Tyre.* New York: Spiral Press, 1963. (Conceived, lettered and illustrated by Shahn.)

Shahn, Ben. *Sweet Was The Song.* New York: Museum of Modern Art, 1956. (Musical score and calligraphy by Shahn.)

Shahn, Ben. *The Alphabet of Creation.* An Ancient Legend from the Zohar. New York: Pantheon, 1954.

Untermeyer, Louise. *Love Sonnets.* New York: The Odyssey Press, 1964.

MONOGRAPHS AND MAJOR EXHIBITION CATALOGUES

Ben Shahn. Amsterdam: Stedelijk Museum, 1962. (Catalogue of exhibition circulated by the International Council of the Museum of Modern Art, December 22, 1961-January 22, 1962.)

Ben Shahn. Brussels: Palais Des Beaux-Arts, 1962. (Catalogue of exhibition circulated by the International Council of the Museum of Modern Art, February 3-25, 1962.)

Ben Shahn. Rome: Galleria Nazionale D'Arte Moderna, 1962. (Catalogue of the exhibition circulated by the International Council of The Museum of Modern Art, March 31-April 29, 1962.)

Ben Shahn. Vienna: Albertina, 1962. (Catalogue of exhibition circulated by the International Council of The Museum of Modern Art, May 22-June 24, 1962.)

Ben Shahn: The Saga of the Lucky Dragon. New York: The Downtown Gallery, 1961. (Catalogue of exhibition of paintings and drawings, October 10-November 4, 1961.)

Golden, Cipe P. *A Medal for Ben.* New York: American Institute of Graphic Arts, 1959. (Remarks delivered by Mrs. Golden at the presentation of the medal of the American Institute of Graphic Arts to Ben Shahn at a dinner meeting in New York, November 13, 1958.)

McNulty, Kneeland (ed.). *The Collected Prints of Ben Shahn.* Philadelphia: Philadelphia Museum of Art, 1967.

Messer, T. M. *Ben Shahn: A Documentary Exhibition.* Boston: Institute of Contemporary Art, 1957. (Mimeographed catalogue of exhibition, April 10-May 31, 1957.)

Ritchie, Andrew C. and Soby, James Thrall (eds.). *Esposizione Biennale Internazionale D'Arte XXVII.* Venice: 1954. (Catalogue of American section, texts in Italian and English, with statements by the artists.)

Rivera, Diego. *The Mooney Case By Ben Shahn.* New York: The Downtown Gallery, 1933. (Catalogue of exhibition of 16 gouaches, May 2-20, 1933.)

Rodman, Selden. *Portrait of the Artist as an American. Ben Shahn: A Biography with Pictures.* New York: Harper, 1951.

Soby, James Thrall. *Ben Shahn.* (The Penguin Modern Painters.) New York: The Museum of Modern Art and Penguin Books, 1947.

Soby, James Thrall. "Ben Shahn." *Museum of Modern Art Bulletin*. (Summer, 1947), 1-47. (Special issue devoted to Shahn retrospective; supplement to the Penguin monograph.)

Soby, James Thrall. *Ben Shahn: His Graphic Art*. New York: George Braziller, 1957.

GENERAL REFERENCES

Barr, Alfred H., Jr. (ed.). *Masters of Modern Art*. New York: The Museum of Modern Art, 1954, 162.

Baur, John (ed.). *New Art in America: Fifty Painters of the 20th Century*. Greenwich, Connecticut: New York Graphic Society in co-operation with Frederick A. Praeger, Inc., New York, 1957, "Ben Shahn," by James Thrall Soby, 118-23; statement by the artist, 123.

Eliot, Alexander. *Three Hundred Years of American Painting*. New York: Time, Inc., 1957, 237, 239-241, 242.

Goodrich, Lloyd and Baur, John. *American Art of Our Century*. New York: Published for the Whitney Museum of American Art by Frederick A. Praeger, Inc., 1961, 101, 158, 163, 165.

Larkin, Oliver. *Art and Life in America*. New York: Rinehart, 1949, 430, 437-438, 441, 465, 466, 476-479.

Pearson, Ralph M. *The Modern Renaissance in American Art*. New York: Harper, 1954, 117-123.

Soby, James Thrall. *Contemporary Painters*. New York: The Museum of Modern Art, 1948, 40-50.

Vollmer, Hans. *Allgemeines Lexikon der bildenden Künstler*. Leipzig, 1958, IV, 268-269.

ARTICLES

"A Tempera and a Drawing by Ben Shahn." *University of Michigan Bulletin*. (May, 1951.)

Abell, Walter. "Art and Labor." *Magazine of Art*. (October, 1946), 231, 235-236, 239, 254-256. (Discusses Shahn's contributions to the CIO Political Action Committee.)

"Angry Eye." *Time*. (October 13, 1947), 63.

Art Digest. (April 15, 1932), 31. (Sacco-Vanzetti series.)

Art Digest. (June, 1951), 19.

Art Digest. (April 1, 1952), 20.

Art Digest. (November 1, 1953), 3.

Art Digest. (February 1, 1955), 22.

Art News. (January, 1948), 36.

Art News. (November, 1949), 44.

Art News. (January, 1950), 13.

Art News. (June, 1951), 47.

Art News. (April, 1952), 45.

Art News. (February, 1955), 56.

Art News. (November, 1955), 17. (Shahn/Baskin: collaboration on the color wood engraving: "Beatitudes.")

81

Art News. (June, 1956), 7.

Art News. (November, 1961), 20.

Arts. (June, 1956), 8.

"Baffling Ben." *Time.* (November 5, 1951), 82.

Baltimore Museum News. (April, 1948), 6.

Barr, Alfred H., Jr. "Gli Stati Uniti alla Biennale: Shahn e de Kooning—Lachaise, Lassaw e Smith." *La Biennale di Venezia.* (April-June, 1954), 62-67.

Barr, Alfred H., Jr. "Portrait: Ben Shahn." *Art In America.* (Winter, 1957-1958), 46-50. (Photographs of the artist at work by Fernandez.)

"Ben Shahn," in "After Hours" [a column]. *Harper's Magazine.* (December, 1957), 79-81. (Discusses Shahn's illustrations for *Harper's* articles.)

"Ben Shahn a Venezia." *Domus.* (September, 1954), 36-37.

"Ben Shahn: The Downtown Gallery." *Art News.* (April 19, 1932), 10. (Review of Sacco-Vanzetti exhibition.)

"Ben Shahn: The Downtown Gallery." *Art News.* (May 13, 1933), 5. (Review of Mooney exhibition.)

"Ben Shahn: Painter of Protest Turns to Reflection." *Life.* (October 4, 1954), 96-100.

"Ben Shahn. Portrait of the Artist No. 182." *Art News and Review.* (January, 1956).

"Bitterness Leavened With Wit." *Art Digest.* (November 1, 1947), 12.

Breuning, Margaret. "Ben Shahn Looks Upon the Seamy Side." *Art Digest.* (December 1, 1944), 17.

Bryson, Bernarda. "The Drawings of Ben Shahn." *Image* [London]. (Autumn, 1949), 31-50. (Includes reproductions of drawings for the CBS programs *Fear Begins at Forty* and *Mind in the Shadow,* and for articles in the *New Republic, Fortune,* and *Harper's.*)

Chamberlain, Betty. "Ben Shahn at the Museum of Modern Art." *Art News.* (October, 1947), 40.

Chanin, A. L. "Shahn, Sandburg of the Painters." *The Sunday Compass.* (October 30, 1949), Magazine, 14.

Charlot, Jean. "Ben Shahn." *Hound and Horn.* (July-September, 1933), 632-634.

Charlot, Jean. "Murals for Tomorrow." *Art News.* (July, 1945), 20.

Coates, Robert M. "Ben Shahn. Exhibition of Paintings and Drawings at The Downtown Gallery." *The New Yorker.* (November 5, 1949), 79-80.

Coates, Robert M. "Contemporary Americans." *The New Yorker.* (October 11, 1947), 64.

Coates, Robert M. "Exhibition at The Downtown Gallery." *The New Yorker.* (January 29, 1955), 54.

Coates, Robert M. "New Show at The Downtown Gallery." *The New Yorker.* (December 2, 1944), 95.

Coates, Robert M. "Should Painters Have Ideas?" *The New Yorker.* (March 14, 1959), 145-155.

Connolly, Cyril. "An American Tragedy." *New Statesman and Nation.* (June 29, 1946), 467-468. (Review of the Tate Gallery exhibition of American art.)

Creative Art. (May, 1932), 396. (Reviews of Sacco-Vanzetti Exhibition at The Downtown Gallery.)

82

Davis, Stuart. "'We Reject'—the Art Commission." *Art Front*. (July, 1935), 4-5. (Protests the rejection of the Riker's Island mural by the Municipal Art Commission; illustrations of a section and a detail of the proposed mural.)

Eliot, Alexander. "Under the Four Winds." *Time*. (June, 1954), 74.

Farr, Dennis. "Graphic Work of Ben Shahn at the Leicester Galleries." *Burlington Magazine*. (December, 1959), 470.

"Five Painters of America." *Worcester Museum News Bulletin*. (March, 1955), 1-4.

Frankel, H. "Glass Houses and Green Rooms." *Saturday Review*. (May 15, 1965), 30.

Gellert, Hugo. "We Captured the Walls!" *Art Front*. (November, 1934), 8. (About the proposed rejection of murals submitted for the Museum of Modern Art exhibition)

Getlein, F. "Art Against the Grain." *Horizon*. (July, 1962), 4, 12-13.

Getlein, F. "Ben Shahn on Fallout." *New Republic*. (November 27, 1961), 20.

Getlein, F. "Letter and the Spirit." *New Republic*. (January 25, 1964), 25-26.

Getlein, F. "$175 Bargain." *New Republic*. (April 30, 1966), 27-28.

Gilroy, Harry. "A Happy Response to Ben Shahn in Amsterdam." *The New York Times*. (January 21, 1962), Section 2, 17. (A report of the exhibition circulated by the International Council of the Museum of Modern Art.)

Golden, Cipe Pineles. "Ben Shahn and the Artist as Illustrator." *Motif*. (September, 1959), 94-95.

Greenberg, Clement. "Art." *The Nation*. (November 1, 1947), 481. (Review of the Museum of Modern Art retrospective.)

Gutman, Walter. "The Passion of Sacco-Vanzetti." *The Nation*. (April 20, 1932), 475. (Review of The Downtown Gallery exhibition.)

Hale, Herbert D. "Ben Shahn." *Art News*. (April, 1959), 13.

Harling, Robert. "Ben Shahn in Roosevelt." *Art*. (June 9, 1955), 2-3.

"Heard at the Galleries." *Pictures on Exhibit*. (November, 1944), 16.

Hess, Thomas B. "Ben Shahn Paints a Picture." *Art News*. (May, 1949), 20-22, 55-56.

Huxtable, Ada Louise. "Designed to Sell." *Art Digest*. (March 1, 1954), 12.

Josephson, Matthew. "Passion of Sacco-Vanzetti." *New Republic*. (April 20, 1932), 275.

Kramer, Hilton. "Month in Review." *Arts*. (April, 1959), 44-45.

Kroll, Jack. *Art News*. (November, 1961), 20.

Lane, James W. "New Pictures by Shahn; Theodore Lux." *Art News*. (May 18, 1940), 11.

Lerman, Leo. "American Eye." *House and Garden*. (December, 1946), 209.

Lionni, Leo. "Ben Shahn, His Graphic Work." *Graphis 62*. (1955), 468-485. (Includes selection from *Paragraphs on Art*; cover of issue by Shahn.)

Look. (July 18, 1950), 70.

Loucheim, Aline B. "Ben Shahn Illuminates." *The New York Times,* (August 30, 1953), Section 2, 8. ("Artist makes drawings for Off-Broadway production of three plays called 'The World of Shalom Aleichem.'")

Loucheim, Aline B. "Shahn Feels Deeply and Sees Clearly." *Art News.* (November 15, 1944), 18-19.

Magazine of Art. (January, 1953), 43.

"Mellowed Militant." *Time.* (September 15, 1967), 73-74.

"Mirrors and Messages." *Time.* (January 31, 1955), 60.

"Modern Art in Advertising: Designs for Container Corporation of America." [Chicago]. (1946.)

"Modern Museum Honors Ben Shahn." Art Digest. (October 15, 1947), 11.

Moe, Ole Henrik. "Ben Shahn." Kunsten Idag. [Oslo]. (November 1, 1956.)

"Mooney Theme." *Art Digest.* (May 1, 1933), 14.

"Morals in Murals." *Art Front.* (July, 1935), 3.

"New Deal Defeatism." *Daily Mirror* [New York]. (October 16, 1944), 17. (Election campaign, anti-Roosevelt editorial using as its starting point Shahn's poster *For Full Employment After The War—Register—Vote.*)

New Theatre. (November, 1934), 18-19. (Scenes from the Living Theatre—Sidewalks of New York: photographs by Ben Shahn.)

"Ohio Magic." *California Palace of the Legion of Honor Bulletin.* (December, 1948), 72.

Paris, George. "Ben Shahn." *Motive.* (March, 1950), 11-16.

Pearson, R. M. "Ben Shahn at the Modern." *Art Digest.* (December 1, 1947), 36.

Peck, Edward S. "Ben Shahn, His 'Personal Statement' in Drawings and Prints." *Impression.* (September, 1957), 6-13.

"1955 Jury of Award for the 1955 Pittsburgh International." *Carnegie Magazine.* (October, 1955), 262.

Preston, M. "Image: Three reviews," *Opera.* (November 27, 1962), 8-12.

Print. (September, 1955), 24.

Rodman, Selden. "Ben Shahn." *Art Digest.* (December 1, 1951), 22.

Rodman, Selden. "Ben Shahn." *Portfolio.* [The Annual of the Graphic Arts]. (1951), 6-21.

Rodman, Selden. "Ben Shahn: Painter of America." *Perspectives USA.* (Fall, 1952), 87-96.

Shahn, Ben. *Current Biography.* (1954), 565-566.

"Shahn Best of 375." *Art Digest.* (November 15, 1940), 8. (Mural competition for the Social Security Building.)

"Sharecroppers . . . seen by the camera eye of Dorothea Lange and Ben Shahn." *Theatre and Film.* (April, 1937), 24-25.

Soby, James Thrall. "Ben Shahn." *Graphis* 22. (1948), 102-107, 188-189.

Soby, James Thrall. "Ben Shahn and Morris Graves." *Contemporary Painters.* (1948), 40-50.

Soby, James Thrall. "Ben Shahn and Morris Graves." *Horizon.* (October, 1947), 48-57.

Stokes, I. N. Phelps. Letter to the editor protesting Philippa Whitings article. *American Magazine of Art.* (October, 1935), 635-637.

"The Bronx—A Typical Treasury Competition." *Art Digest.* (June 1, 1938), 26.

"The Third Allegory." *Jewish Center News.* [Buffalo]. (April, 1956).

Werner, Alfred. "Ben Shahn." *Reconstructionist.* (October 3, 1958), 16, 19-22.

Werner, Alfred. "Ben Shahn's Magic Line." *The Painter and Sculptor.* (Spring, 1959), 1-4.

Whiting, Philippa. "Speaking About Art: Riker's Island." *American Magazine of Art.* (August, 1935), 492-496.

"Whitman Censored." *Art Digest.* (January 1, 1939), 14.

Wilenski, R. H. "A London Look at U.S. Painting in the Tate Gallery Show." *Art News.* (August, 1946), 23-29. (Refers to Shahn's *Liberation.*)

Woolfenden, William E. "Composition for Clarinets and Tin Horn." *Detroit Institute of Arts Bulletin.* 1952-1953), 20-21.

INDEX